C000101691

Growing Up

The result

NASRO MOHAMUUD

authorHOUSE®

AuthorHouse™ UK
1663 Liberty Drive
Bloomington, IN 47403 USA
www.authorhouse.co.uk
Phone: 0800.197.4150

© 2015 Nasro Mohamuud. All rights reserved.

No part of this book may be reproduced, stored in a retrieval system, or
transmitted by any means without the written permission of the author.

Published by AuthorHouse   02/10/2016

ISBN: 978-1-5049-9181-0 (sc)
ISBN: 978-1-5049-9182-7 (e)

Print information available on the last page.

Any people depicted in stock imagery provided by Thinkstock are
models, and such images are being used for illustrative purposes only.
Certain stock imagery © Thinkstock.

This book is printed on acid-free paper.

Because of the dynamic nature of the Internet, any web
addresses or links contained in this book may have changed
since publication and may no longer be valid. The views
expressed in this work are solely those of the author and do
not necessarily reflect the views of the publisher, and the
publisher hereby disclaims any responsibility for them.

Acknowledgments

I would like to say thank you to God for able to make my dream of becoming author true.

Furthermore I would like to say thank you to my family and friends who always surprises me and supports me.

To you

mother

Contents

My team

I love you

I care about you

I need you

I want you

I like you

I like you

I love you

I follow you

I am your child

I am your student

I am your loved one

You, I love you.

One mother with one baby girl

I love you!

Today

I am living now

My future is now

The past has gone

My past is filled in my eyes with a great living

I live my life knowing I live it to the fullest

I make no mistakes

So, why should I worry about the past?

The past has gone

If I sinned in the past, I ask forgiveness from the lord

I live now

I am grateful for now

This is now

And about my future, I will say it when the present becomes the past.

I live knowing I am happy

Coughing

The sound of coughing through my throat

So much pain

The sound going right through my ears

So loud that it is affecting my chest

Painful it is

I want it to go away

But it's not going away

It's so hard

What will i do?

I have taken every thing

I don't understand what it is

Doctors don't understand it either

I wish I understand what it is

It leaves me with a painful memory

A memory which is hard to remember

I think it's a mild infection

But how did I contract it?

Every time a bit of cold occurs, I catch it

One day, I wore a coat which my sister asked me to buy.

But every time my niece catches cold, I get it

I think, know or believe I will go and see a doctor again.

I hope when the doctor sees me and says it's an infection he can make it go away

Feelings

I build it with knowledge

I am making a relationship

I am caring

I love

Feelings that feel good are good

Feel excellent

Feel proud

Feel special

Feel enjoyment

Feel genius

Feel what you want

Feel free

Feel together

Think being without each other absence

Know what you want

Like me first

Love me and be happy

Enjoy

Flowers

You must think what do the flowers got to do with anything?

My reply, I just can't help

But like flowers, I think about flowers all day long

They make me wonder off to another world,
a world which is great and everything smells good

I just can't help but like flowers to bring to my home and share
with others.

I am sure if people saw what I see, they would have been sold.
I mean I like them just the way they are
You must know which one is your favourite

I want you to know I have no favourite

I like every one of them

I can't help but like flowers with pink colour which smell fresh.

Hurting words

Words misused are often hurtful

They can hurt one very badly

I hear them saying these words out loudly

From even parents to their children

Even when one is a grown-up

Words such as you've never grown up are hurtful

And can bring damage to a person's mind

They surely do say hurting words to me

I don't understand why they won't leave me alone

But I hear them all the time

11

Good words

Words said right can make a difference in my life and the world

Words are powerful; the power of life and death is in the tongue.

It's my life and my world and I love good words

Please try to get rewards and use good words

I love words because their ability is magic

And I like magic

Words such us I am proud of you can make one win

And I do like to be a winner.

Friends

Few of you really do like other people

But I am not the one who seems to keep you according to your means

So very many of you left me

And some threaten me

But are you not scared of having friends?

I mean friends are rear

And I am one who does something meaningful

The lord is my friend

And

God has never left me

Or threatened me

Or said I am not good enough

Or my home wasn't clean

Or I was not cool enough

God loves me for whom I am

And I know that through prayer

I don't like your lies

So please don't be friends with me

And if you can find space in your heart for friends please do

Or you will regret.

My life is too great for deserters

I only invite those who have my interest at their bosom

My style

I like certain style

But the powerful just don't understand

They claim they are too powerful for my style

They make me feel I want something from them

But thanks to God for I have all I want

I am so powerful I don't even need to hear disappointments

They always correct me

But I know they are correcting someone else

Because I know my style is good

People try to correct my clothes' style

My writing style, my business style

Correction must be their best job

And you must have a job called corrector

Please stay away from correcting me

Because my style has been work effective

For your information I am successful

The white plan

This is what I said about people

Whom no one can please

One stupid person

Following a stupid plan

Powered by stupid people

With stupid power

Coming with stupid ideas

Trying to be taken over by stupid ideas

A person with stupid thoughts

With weak strength

Behind them stupid group

In a stupid state of mind

Good then, the result you have is insane

So stop coming with stupid thoughts

You are a stupid person

Whom no one can please?

Bad girl

She never listens because listening is too hard for her

She never smiles back because she has never had someone to look up to

She worships the wrong person

Her parents never worshipped anyone either

The little respect she can find is in her items

She has a sharp mouth

And her key to success Is to bring success through doubt

She is controlled, so she wants these people to control her

But one finds them too dirty

She has an eye to my state

And has a force which is a dictator

And half of the city is scared of them

Her favourite thing to do is the use of physical abuse

I think she is gossiped by everyone inviting her

But half of the city is afraid of them

It's not the right thing but it's addictive

Because she is a joke

Who is she?

She is the one trying to be friendly with you

Whom no one wants

Her name is the one we all know

We don't know anything about him but we can't see her dropping by in our sitting room

Genus

Who is really a genius?

I believe a genius is someone who has actualized

Someone who knows something no one knows

Someone who knows what supreme God means

A genius knows between the right thing and wrong thing

A genius is someone who knows how to stay away from problems.

A genius is someone who stays away from abusive friendship

A genius is someone who knows she is lucky in marriage

A genius is someone who never hurts others.

A genius is someone who knows their parent's state

A genius is someone with a religion and gets the highest reward.

A genius is someone who has reached a high level in the society while he or she is an adult

A genius is someone who never fights and when one gets angry leaves the room

Last but not least genius is grateful for his ingenuity.

Help

Help is difficult to get

Refusing to help the great, is unnecessary these days

Because they want to be on top them

Through watching TV and being busy with their mobile

They heard voices refusing to give help

Because it's not paying enough

But if I can't pay enough,

Who could?

I personally like others to get help when they need it

I gave help when I was younger

And I thought that was great!

Seeing people big made me want to be bigger

But again, if you can't see your success who can see it

That is what you will be one day?

I don't know who refuses help and need

Personally, I think you are making people pay because you never had help.

Bravery

I guess bravery is important; at least I would like to know

Because everything in life I do I have to own bravery.

I guess bravery is hard to possess but every time I need bravery,

I think of never being taken a fool decision.

I think this is so because I've never trusted any wrong decision

I believe any trust it's because I watch what I want and demand understanding

I guess that's because I follow the wisdom I have gained through the years.

I guess I never trusted anyone to make a decision for me because I am able to make my own decision for myself.

I mean not joking, I am sound so I take my decision and if you ask me it takes bravery.

I write this because I've come across someone who I trust to take an important decision that concerns me. I don't know how I will trust him but, I know I will count on myself. I pray to God that I succeed because, good luck never harms me.

Refusing me

You think you are more than me

But in life you have to calculate and balance

And if you have done me bad, I am better than you

You don't deserve me or others either

Aren't people supposed to be equal?

Why do you refuse me?

For your information, I never wanted you

Because am better than you

You lost your self

Because you left yourself when you left me

Who is keeping a record?

You think you are better than me?

But I am better than you

You wasted time of your youth

You also tried to waste the time of your childhood

But they all grow up

And I have God looking after me

And I promise I will stay away from you

School

I always thought of doing my best in education

But some other people in my school

Thought learning was a competitive

Could have most friendships or the best handwriting

But as I was prepared to do my best in school, because I knew I would achieve high if I did my best and to me it seemed the ones who were concerned with others then education was

Allowed to get ahead

As I am older now and I look back, I could only look back with happiness

And I could look back as I did my best and that puts smiles on my face.

I didn't worry about pleasing someone else

However it did matter to me to look good

And I suppose I did.

Now as I am older, I know I have achieved high

Not many people have jobs

But I have my education and that keeps me going.

I know I have achieved something because I am able to diagnose

I am also able to express myself in writing how important it was for me to know I was right

Education is more important than anything.

Today, I look back with happiness and I wonder in my mind and ask myself what could I have I done without my education?

I celebrate for learning

And I am very happy I did concentrate on education.

This age

Today is not an old age or even the golden age

It is the 21st age

Age when the girls are stronger than anyone

Age when what we see in the world is more advanced than any age

But again as they say, with time you advance

I sure do like advance

But I ask myself how next age will could have more than us.

I am sure I made their life a better than today

I don't know how that is possible

But I think they will know how great this time was

I think in time I will advance

Because I still don't know how heaven is.

Nature

So beautiful, so great

So colourful, so organized

Well put together

Enjoyment for my eyes

Such a nice smell

Water, trees, skies, desert, mountains, oceans

Few of my favourite

What would have happened without the idea of forever living without nature?

About love

Experience thought me love is great

Love is unique and love is highly valued

I say this is what love is all about.

The far we have reached is as a result of love between us

Love did define as all along

Love is what I have known

The love we created in the past is the love I am talking about

I love you!

Love is saying I love you when I just met you

Love you baby for being there for our relationship to grow

I am saying, I love you once again

O love myself and you together

So let's have together something special

Take a gift from me so huge that you will never be able to rest

I have a gift for you too

I know you have too

But for now, I will wait for you

As you wait, know I love you

My sides

My sides

I have many sides

That's me

I have many sides

I have many looks

That's me

I have many looks

My fashion is diverse

That's me

I have much fashion

I have many ways

That's me

My ways are many

God made me beautiful

I share the world with so many people

Many of them have seen how look

And I like it

When I write,

I mean they know about me

Because one day, I hope many other sides of a person will go away.

I like my sides because God made with love

I hope just as I know my many sides

I will appreciate them and keep liking them

My sides are many

That's me

I have many sides

Others like my looks

However, I appreciate them

Because that is the best of me

I have many looks

That's me

My looks are many

I know I have many sides

Because every time I see my self

Or look at myself in the mirror,

I see a new look

When I was young, I tried to memorize how I look on the mirror

But now I realize I first need to memorize how I see myself: gorgeous.

The ugly truth I see is not me; it's the observation of what some think of me

They are those who wasted their life risk doing

Others were unjust to me by

Committing crimes of not telling the whole truth

My beauty

I sometimes wonder why I don't seem to see the whole truth in front of me

I came to the idea these times we are told we might be free and in fact I think we are free

But who is really accepting me for my own beautiful girl I am?

According to me if they did I know some will get over their meanness

And start to appreciate me for all I am

They will start to love me for God's sake

Only then they will start to have what they are looking for and that's is I love God and

My beauty comes from there and so is my fortune.

Unlike the people full of opinions

I fear shame because my knowledge

I know you are full of yourself because of the way your words are so much

You talk to me about my home

My clothes

My abilities

But who are you really?

Whatever you thinking of now to tell me

I am above that and yes I have friends

I have no time for temporary friendship because

I have the friendship of those I love

And one day the cherry on top

One day I will be having friendship of God.

Lightning Source UK Ltd.
Milton Keynes UK
UKOW04f0141080316

269799UK00001B/2/P